MANCHESTER AND *Beyond*
-POEMS

POEMS FROM MANCHESTER

STEPHEN SUTTON

authorHOUSE

AuthorHouse™ UK
1663 Liberty Drive
Bloomington, IN 47403 USA
www.authorhouse.co.uk
Phone: UK TFN: 0800 0148641 (Toll Free inside the UK)
UK Local: 02036 956322 (+44 20 3695 6322 from outside the UK)

© 2020 Stephen Sutton. All rights reserved.

No part of this book may be reproduced, stored in a retrieval system, or transmitted by any means without the written permission of the author.

Published by AuthorHouse 10/28/2020

ISBN: 978-1-6655-8144-8 (sc)
ISBN: 978-1-6655-8161-5 (e)

Print information available on the last page.

Any people depicted in stock imagery provided by Getty Images are models, and such images are being used for illustrative purposes only.
Certain stock imagery © Getty Images.

This book is printed on acid-free paper.

Because of the dynamic nature of the Internet, any web addresses or links contained in this book may have changed since publication and may no longer be valid. The views expressed in this work are solely those of the author and do not necessarily reflect the views of the publisher, and the publisher hereby disclaims any responsibility for them.

MANCHESTER

Manchester is known throughout the world for its football teams Manchester united and Manchester city, but its also known for its three universities namely Manchester university, Manchester Metropolitan university and Salford university all of which offers the best education. I have had the honour of attending two of them and accomplished work for the other, my time at Salford was the more memorable as I graduated and became a qualified nurse.

There are many places to visit Museums, art galleries and pubs. The city is alive with activity and the people of Manchester have proven they can pull together in a crises such as the Manchester bombing at the Arndale shopping centre, the Ariana Grande Concert when many lives were lost and youths injured in a suicide bombing, followed by the one love concert. Not forgetting gay Manchester pride held in August when people acknowledge equality and diversity and supporting the gay community, take a trip to Canal Street to the popular bars and hospitality there.

Manchester has a lot more to offer in the way of talent such as great musicians, artists, poets and novelists and song writers/ performers such as Oasis, the Bee Gees, Davy Jones of the Monkees and many more, these have been recognised for their fine work people like David

Arnot known for his magnificent Mosaics. Poets such as Carl Anthony Waldron these are the people who deserve praise and admiration for their fine efforts. This book is designed to focus on local and distant talent from Manchester and beyond, specifically from all over the world. Speaking as a poet, artist and novelist I am proud to share my poetry with others in this book as they have shared them with me. People from Manchester and beyond, all over the world who truly appreciate poetry and art, so many creative people I reach out to you where ever you are, Manchester greets you with open arms, share your talent with us.

I want to take this opportunity to mention a photographer called Matthew Fychan who is well known for his work in Manchester. His work is displayed in this book providing aspects of his superb work.

ACKNOWLEDGEMENTS

I wish to thank all the poets who have contributed to this book for their fine work and very kind gesture, it means a great deal to me to have so many writers involved who have all given their permission to have their poems in my book and the credit going to them of course. I must say that this book is dedicated to Carl Anthony Waldron who passed away this year he will be sadly missed, Carl was an ex police officer who had a great talent in writing poetry and songs for Ashton lane, some of his work is featured in my book. I want to thank my brave girl Gemma Louise Sutton for her front line work as a NHS mental health nurse, for my daughter Jeni Sutton for supporting me along with my son's Michael and Daniel.

FRONT COVER ARTIST
STEVEN ROBERT BRUCE

Steven Robert Bruce born 1956 and raised in Ashton-under-Lyne schools- Parochial junior school and Ashton grammar senior school.

took art as one of my subjects but failed o'level. I was a hairdresser until moving to Blackpool in 1997. I began painting by chance in 1994 at the age of 38 when my then partner gave me an oil painting starter kit for my birthday. My obsession started right there and am a self taught artist.

I took a job as a postman with royal mail in 2001 to give myself more time for painting in the afternoons, eventually taking medical retirement in December 2013. Since then I have painted full time.

2014 I created my website and started having prints done of my art. I won a prize at Lytham arts festival 2014

in 2016 I held a successful solo exhibition at Stockport War Memorial and Art Gallery.

2018 I was featured as February artist of the month in the magazine Lancashire Life and July2018 I won Blackpool Winter Gardens 140th Anniversary art comp.

since 2014 I have regularly held exhibitions locally at the pavilion cafe in St Anne's. I am on twitter as @bruceyart and facebook as 'Steven Bruce artist' and instagram as matblack8

I have two children and 8 grandchildren.

Ashton Under Lyne Greater Manchester
painted in colour 1963

Matthew Fychan photographer from Manchester tells me
'I have aspergers/high function autism, it makes me think far too deeply about simple questions'. He was happy to be part of this book; he has contributed with

Aspects of Manchester by Matthew Fychan

CONTENTS

All Lives Matter 1
Depression...2
Childs Play 3
Child Slave 4
He Drowned Me 6
Me And My Selves...7
In Our Darkest Days 9
"For King And Country" 11
Manchester Talent 12
Manchester Prison (Strange Ways) 14
The Mancunian 15
"Manchester Oh Manchester"..16
One Love Manchester 18
United In Grief...20
Manchester Pride 22
City Life 24
Nathaniel 26
Grieving 27
The Wild Child..28
Believe Me 29
Injustice 30
So Profound...31
Crippled World 32
Crowded Places 34
Demonstation 35
A Lover's Quest 37

Nobody Listens	39
When I Fall	41
Reflections	43
Into Darkness	44
Moral Guidance	45
Lock Down	48
Prayer For Recovery	49
Pandemic	50
Living A Complex Life	52
Buiding Your Life With A Solid Foundation	53
Helpless	55
Faded Light	56
Psychic	57
Living In A Box	58
The Love That Never Was	60
Padded Cell	62
Witches	63
Waking Blind	64
Exposure To Love	65
Senseless Words	66
Naked	68
Calm Waters	69
Fill The Earth With Pagans	70
Ancient Ruins	71
Dream On	73
Those Eyes	74
Profound Thoughts	75
Freedom From Bondage	76
Whimpered	77
Lee	78

The Lonely Night Watchman	83
Substance Recluse	84
Birth And Death	85
Tormenting Spirit	86
Africa	87
Transformation	88
Show Me	89
Riptide	91
Goodbye Africa	93
Immigrant Girl	95
The Darkest Of Days	96
Courage	97
Silent World	99
Multi Colours	101
Home Before Dark	103
Faded Light	104
Portrait Of My Soul	105
Rescue Me	107
Living With A Phobia	108
The Effects Of Fear	109
Grieving	111
The Reality Of Mental Health	113
Let The Candles Burn	118
All Or Nothing	119
My Brave Girl (Gemma)	120
My Perfect Woman	121
Gender Crises	122
Scars	124
Hopeless Mess	125
My Friend The Bottle	128

Diary Of A Teenage Drug Addict............................130
Damage 132
The Wilderness 134
Bipolar...137
Who Am I 139
Do You See Me 140
Life Is Beautiful 142
Look 145
Thoughts And Prayers..146
Step 147
Mr. Sutton 148
Transition (The Link)...149
The Ghost..150
The Slug That Ate My Lettuce 152
The Biddy Mobile 153
Walking My Hamster...155
Childhood Stress 157
Like Angels Do 159
Nothing Is Real (Part 2) 160
Manchester Air 162
The Manchester Busker 163
Sad Meal 165
Journey Through The Mind Of A Killer 166
Love Without Boundary.......................................167
Voice Of The Dead...168
Westward The Sirocco Winds Of Pluto March.......170

ALL LIVES MATTER

by Stephen Robert Sutton

Black lives matter
We know this is true
When we are caged in
Like animals in a zoo

Frustrated by our system
That is the case
Living like slaves
In our human race

But every life matters
All colour and creed
Don't live like the rich folk
Governed by greed

Live life in harmony
Do what is best
Share all your love
And damn all the rest

Freedom is important
With no slavery
Fighting for justice
Live in harmony

DEPRESSION

by Morganna Avalon

Woke up this morning feeling bad--
People said its ok, you're only sad--
A thousand times I've slashed my wrists in my head--
A hundred more wishing I was dead--

Blood dripping onto the floor--
Oozing out till there is no more--
A crimson stain at my feet--
Popping pills in the street--

Trapped in a prison i call my home--
Sometimes feels im so alone--
No-one sees the pain i try to hide--
No-one knows how i feel inside--

Gotta get out of this place, slap a smile on
--Hey do you think anyone will notice today--
It's all a con?

copyright..M.Avalon (2019)

CHILDS PLAY

by Stephen Robert Sutton

Taking all my children
All around the park
Playing on the swings
Singing like a lark

Sitting in the park
Watching everyone
Lying on the grass
Basking in the sun

Splashing in the water
Playing in the sand
Going down the slide
I give a helping hand

Happy children
Shout away
Tired by the
End of day

Night time comes
It's time for bed
Time top rest
Weary head

CHILD SLAVE

by Stephen Robert Sutton

Don't treat your child this way
You work her hard each day
By giving her chore
Both in and out doors

Don't treat your child this way

Making them work instead of play
This is definitely not the way
Give them the freedom to move around
Don't make them mute without making a sound

Don't treat your child this way
I beg you don't treat the child this way

Making them wash the floor
Scrub the bathroom and much more
Sending them off to the shops
This child slavery never stops

Don't treat the child this way
I implore you
Don't treat the child this way

Don't make your child a slave
I ask you to behave

Let them grow as a child
Not to be reckless or wild
This is a fact this is the truth
Let them play happily in their youth

HE DROWNED ME

by Autumn Shruggs

Love that four letter word that requires attention.
For I have drowned in these Words.
I have loved so hard, and fought
That I loss myself.

He drowned me, he dammed me to hell,
He hit me I thought this was love.
I laid there an accepted my faith for
I had nothing left to give. I loss myself
For that four letter word.

He protected me, and also rejected me
I wasn't good enough for thee.
Why did He continuously drown me?

I started to drown myself for attention
I cut myself for pleasure, he laughed
He cared not for me, he wanted to
All along drown me.

Copyright © Autumn Scruggs | Year Posted 2020

Life struggles hope u enjoy

ME AND MY SELVES

by Stephen Robert Sutton

How do I start to explain?
About my life when I was sane
Was it real or was it not
To be honest I have almost forgot

About the trauma and the pain
And about the day I went insane
The brutal things that happened to me
I was once in captivity then set free

My mind was whole and now it's apart
Like the chambers of my heart
First I am Frank, and then I am John
How I wish I was only one

So many people in one head
Am I Alan or am I now Fred
One moment a boy then I am a man
Trying to reason as much as I can

My mind is so split I can't see the truth
Why was I abused in my youth?
These people protect me those in my head
The only time I am free is when I am in bed

Sleeping so soundly away from all fear
Till someone disturbs me coming so near
Me and my selves conflicting in thought
Tussling in my brain that life is so short

In the evening the child comes along
To tell me a story or sing me a song
And then in came Frank to protect me from harm
Or Fred to keep me quite calm

My personalities are so different you see
But at time I wish they would let me be
It's confusing because why I must share?
All these people, oh what do I care?

IN OUR DARKEST DAYS

In our darkest of days, Hollow Eyes
What lies beneath these hollow eyes?

We look to the skies.
No elegant beauty,
Nor fading of heart.
In the quietening of spirits We're drifting apart.
What can we gain,
And what can be lost?
Is there life in these depths
Or the passing across?
Will salvation answer on the uprising sun,
Or will God smile and beckon you, 'Come.'
From the tiniest of seed
To the strongest of flower,
From the crumbling stone wall
To the mightiest tower,
Please don't give in.
Don't give up the fight,
As the morning is calling,
Surviving the night.
The brightest star in heaven is having its say.
Down come Gods angels to take you away.
Alas,
The toughest of decisions
That should never be made,
As they switch off the machine And your eyes start to fade.

Tears will fall,
But memories don't die.
Now, just like the angels,
You'll look down from the sky, But not with hollow eyes,
Nor under these false pretences, Nor being enslaved Inside technology's fences.
Away you'll soar
Through the moonlit bay,
In the valleys of heaven,
No torment to pay.
And there you'll climb the candle lit mast, In elegance and beauty.
At peace at last
Jack Tomlinson ©

Please spare a thought for all our Soldiers, men and women, who are out there protecting us this Christmas time.
And please say a Prayer for all those who have laid down their lives for Our country in the past.
Thankyou
Private Wilfred Wood VC
From Stockport, Manchester.

"FOR KING AND COUNTRY"

My name is private Wilfred Wood
I came from Hazel Grove
I snipered from the trenches
I marched through sand and cove
I fought for King and Country
My rifle it stayed true
My VC cross shines for the men
Who lost their lives for you
We stood upon the battlefields
Each soldier young and brave
We fired into the hillsides
We trudged through muddy grave
We fought for King and Country
In Italy near Rome
Red poppies grow for all the men
Who never made it Home
I came home hailed a hero
To tunes of marching bands
I cried for all my comrades
Who'd died in far off lands
We fought for King and Country
Until your War was won
Red poppies bleed for all the folk
Who lost their soldier son
FREEDOM is a virtue
It can take a Man to War
FREEDOM is a lonely road
That We March On Evermore.

By **Carl Anthony Waldron**

MANCHESTER TALENT

by Stephen Robert Sutton

As I look around Manchester
What do I find?
So much talent
It blows my mind

Such gifted people
And that's the truth
So much talent
In all our youth

Artist, musicians, writers
So many to find
Some that are homeless
Many you will find

People of all ages
With promising skills
So much creativity
It gives me the chills

Look at this city
See what you have got
Many fine crafts
They have the lot

Manchester's heritage
The talents are rich
Look at their work
And what they accomplish

So just recognise them
Just take a glance
Let them show you their talent
Please give them a chance

MANCHESTER PRISON (STRANGE WAYS)

by Stephen Robert Sutton

How odd me thinks
The strange bleak place
Where thieves and rogues do go
To think of things of yesterday
Or strange ways if you must know

Manchester prison was once known
By its in mates and officers too
Strange ways was just the place
Where prisoners were welcomed to

A tower stood with a watchful guard
Watching a prisoner escape in plight
They watched him leave and knew for well
The police would catch him later at night

The prison warden paced up and down
Keeping a watchful eye
The prisoners were clear what to do
As they stole the governors pie

What was best there for the rest
Than fifteen years or a five year stretch
Doing your porridge fulfilling the time
Doing your penance for doing the crime

THE MANCUNIAN

by Stephen Robert Sutton

The Mancunian stands tall and proud
The Mancunian is very loud
He stands up for what he believes
And is proud of what he achieves

The Mancunian is so very bright
The Mancunian can put up a fight
He defends those all around
A Mancunian stands his ground

A Mancunian is proud to be
Part of his society
Standing tall standing lean
Support his football team

The Mancunian may be rich or maybe poor
He may appear at your front door
Laughing and joking with all around
It's not unusual just profound

The Mancunian remains tall and proud
He also remains very loud
He is outspoken just like the rest
But he remains one of the best

"MANCHESTER OH MANCHESTER"

It doesn't really matter
If you're a red or blue
And we don't give a dam
If your rains soak us through
We love our northern city
Where everyone stands tall
We love our northern city
We're united till we fall.
Manchester Oh Manchester
Please play a song for me
You're in my blood
You're in my bones
And set my Spirit free
It doesn't really matter
If you're a black or white
And we don't give a dam
If you're a wrong or right
We love our northern city
Through its good times and pain
We love our northern city
Through its sunshine and its rain.
It doesn't really matter
On religion or your faith
And we don't give a dam
If you're a beggar or a waif
We love our northern city

And our battles will be won
We love our northern city
And our Bees that make us one.
Manchester Oh Manchester
Please play a song for me
You're in my blood
You're in my bones
And set my Spirit free

Manchester Oh Manchester
Please play a song for me
You're in my blood
You're in my bones
And set my Spirit free.
God Bless all our Mancy Bees this Christmas time.
May they all rest in peace xxx

And God bless Carl Anthony Waldron for his poems and song which will be remembered, following his untimely death in 2020. One of his songs were performed by Ashton Lane called Barefoot Madonna about Joan Baez

Carl Anthony Waldron
I wrote a poem in honour of Our great City and Our beautiful Bees.

ONE LOVE MANCHESTER

by Stephen Robert Sutton

If ever I was emotional
It was seeing a concert occur
I watched the performers
And suddenly my eyes would blur

Top performers sang their tune
Giving freely of their time
For those who died so senselessly
Isn't it such a crime?

Some where over the rainbow
Was Ariana Grande's song
She sang it so beautifully
With not a single note wrong

People hugged all over town
So many people cried
Flowers lay in the street
For all who had died

One love concert for Manchester
And the cities great despair
What an incredible atmosphere
Love was in the air

So remember one love Manchester
Keep it in your heart
For this city came together
And will never part

Following the horrific time of the terrorist attack in Manchester arena MEN 22nd May 2017 at the Ariana Grande concert, a concert was held on 4th June 2017 in memory of those who died called the 'one love concert' Ariana Grande returned to host this with many celebrity guests in Manchester cricket ground.

UNITED IN GRIEF

by Stephen Robert Sutton

I remember thee
At the sadness of the day
I stand and pray
Where the flower lay

Where people come
Across the street not murmuring a sound
The quietness showing respect
Tragedy they found

The senseless murder of local folk
It's such a senseless crime
Blown away and left for dead
Cut off in their prime

But all of you from Manchester
Witness an event so brief
Mourning side by side
United in your grief

People come and help them
Helping those in need
By giving of themselves
With courage they succeed

A concert is arranged
Raising money to help the cause
Showing solidarity
And a reason to end terrorist wars

MANCHESTER PRIDE

by Stephen Robert Sutton

Experience the rainbow
And support them if you may
No matter what's your sexuality
Being straight or being gay

Join the large procession
Travelling down the street
Transsexuals and all kinds
People you must meet

Manchester pride is happening
All those that count today
Demonstrate their freedom
And their right to be gay

They dress in many colours
Like a rainbow in the sky
Stand and cheer them onward
As they wave and pass you by

Canal Street is alive
It is a bustling place
The queens of Manchester
Never look out of place

So join the pride of Manchester
With their banners flying high
And the rainbows of this world
Will shine in the sky

CITY LIFE

by Stephen Robert Sutton

Hustle bustle on the street
Loud sound from heavy feet
Cars that bleep their horn
Heavy traffic in the morn

People hurry for the train
Rushing pushing and don't explain
Greedy people eat their food
Often people are being rude

Fumes from petrol fill the air
Often people just don't care
Homeless people on the street
With damp wet blankets beneath their feet

Street performers play away
Playing music through the day
Singers with guitars in hand
Playing away like a Mancunian band

Shoppers are looking
For bargains or treats
Children are busy
Filling their faces with sweets

Stands selling hot dog
Trams move all around
Fountains are flowing
In Piccadilly gardens
The people are sound

NATHANIEL

by S.D.Kilmer

Dedicated to my son, Nathaniel
Once I tried to soften the blow, to say
"It is not your fault I must leave, you know!"
In those moments a son needs his father and to play,
For certain these words were lost in the silent response
When you cried out, "Daddy! Daddy!" in the midst of the day.
I did come around, if you recall.
Perhaps never enough of me did you see.
Probably seemed there was between us a great wall.
Only two actions in my life have I deeply regretted.
Both having kept you from me.
But in your eighteenth year, you phoned
And I came in a flash.
It seemed that you were sincere
Perhaps it is true, you only wanted the cash.
Because of your subsequent silence my dear
Brings to remembrance that day I tried to soften the blow.
When I call out from the depth of my thoughts of you, "Nathaniel! Nathaniel!" I know your pain of fatherlessness because
I hear the same you once heard in reply.
The silence that can only invoke me to cry.
Copyright (c) 2019 *HeardWords America.*
S.D.Kilmer

GRIEVING

I'm sitting there contemplating
my eyes filling up with tears
I remember all those memories
we shared over the years.
As I lie there wide awake
I'm staring into space
the images in my head
are of your beautiful face
I'm feeling empty, sad & lonely
emotions I can't control
feelings I've never had before
in my heart you've left a hole.
Even though I know its true
they say that I am grieving
I cannot help the fact
that I am disbelieving.
I'm feeling so hurt
feeling angry deep inside
You couldn't possibly imagine
how many tears I've cried.
They say that times a healer
that you will start to be okay
I know that is not the truth
whichever year or day
By DJT
Image 3
by Demi Tilsley

THE WILD CHILD

Broken and battered
Free and wild
A girl with a burden
Or a rule breaking child

Am I making memories
Or trying to forget
Is this a bad habit
Or my first cigarette

Your opinion is your own
But tell me what you see
Is it sympathy or disgust
When you look at me

My eyes are tired
My hair is ratty
My dress is clean
My stance is bratty

My sister looks on
Hands at her hips
I ignore the show behind me
Pull my rebellion to my lips

By Kelsey LeDel Swiger

BELIEVE ME

by Stephen Robert Sutton

What do you believe?
Does it feel real?
Is it a god?
How does it feel?

When do you worship
When do you pray?
Is it in the morning?
At the end of the day

What do you call him?
Has he a name
Is he glorified?
Due to his fame

Is he a messiah?
A guru or king
A Buddha or Mohammed
Or any old thing

Is he so powerful?
Surrounded by fire
Is he supreme
And one you admire

My look at various religions and beliefs of today, where I ask myself why are there so many religions and what makes people follow such teachings.

INJUSTICE

by Stephen Robert Sutton

What you see is in your head
The person you see alas is dead
You think what you do is right
But all it is, is a racist fight

Don't you see we have a right to live?
And it shows by the love we give
We pray to the same god above
And all we want is love

What we see is injustice I say
When all we want to do is pray
Pray for the weak and feeble in mind
I beg you don't be cruel but be kind

Don't judge a man by his skin
But look at the man within
He bleeds red blood like you and I
So don't make his family cry

At the injustice that you create
Or you surly deserve the same fate
One bad deed to end the day
By your reckless act, by your display

SO PROFOUND

by Stephen Robert Sutton

My life is complex I have often found
It's twists and turns and is so profound
It is a marvel to me that I am still here
Living my life without any fear

I take all the risks in life you see
And pattern my life like an old tapestry
Working out ways to get through the day
And say all the things that I want to say

I intensely think out my hourly chores
I know what is mine and I know which is yours
I keep all my possessions close to my chest
And choose who I want for a guest

I have flown so high into the clouds
Amidst the silence over the crowds
Now I keep my feet close to the ground
And think of something so profound

A loose philosophic look at life with a profound look at logic

CRIPPLED WORLD

by Stephen Robert Sutton

Look at the wars
The famine and disease
Are you ashamed?
Are you displeased?

Global warming
Out of control
A crippled world
The world as a whole

Fear of the madness
Living in shame
Is this world a joke
Are we playing a game

Riots and looting
Pointless pursuits
While politicians
Dress up in their suits

Blinded by opinion
Racism and greed
If you cut yourself
Don't you just bleed?

One mucked up world
Crippled within
Isn't it dreadful?
A global sin

So work together
Don't dither or roam
Repair all the cracks
Make it your home

CROWDED PLACES

by Stephen Robert Sutton

No spaces on the buses
No room on the trains
Too many people round me
You would think they had no brains

I hate such crowded places
No room to sit or breath
This is why I get so anxious
I really want to leave

I push my way through crowds
And run to a quiet place
To gather up my courage
For the journey I must face

The madness of the people
Rushing through the masses
People caught up by the turn styles
With their railway passes

Going through the markets
Madness everywhere
Pushing through the crowds
People never care

DEMONSTATION

by Stephen Robert Sutton

The crowd all gathered
And marched down the street
With lighted torches
And banners with slogans
Made from a sheet

With penned in frustration
Let out in anger you see
The angry crowd are
Coming towards me

Some breaking away
Burning vehicles, breaking things apart
Looting the shops
And leaving their mark

An innocent girl
Is injured on the way
Making her one of many
By the end of the day

The police form a line
For a defence
Attacked by bottles and missiles
Causing offence

One man is left bleeding
In the street all alone
Lying there dead
Holding his phone

The last text he made
To his wife it said
I love you dear
And then he was dead

A LOVER'S QUEST

I have searched horizons far and wide,
And trecked the sands of time,
Sailed seven seas,
And chased four winds,
In hope that She'd be mine.
I have sat upon the moon on high,
And slept on clouds above,
Tiptoed through stars,
Jumped Venus and Mars,
In hope to gain Her love.
I have prayed to God on bended knee,
Soared with Angels in the sky,
Danced with Devil,
And sold my soul,
In hopes to hear Her sigh.
I have climbed all hill and mountainside,
Followed every map and chart,
Crossed desert plains,
And all terrains,
In hope to win Her heart

Have You Ever Written a Poem?
Tony Longfella Walsh is apparently our renowned and acclaimed Poet of Manchester.
But there are many other poets out there within our fantabulous City.

Including homeless people and buskers etc etc etc.
I myself am fortunate not to be any of the above, but some say I can write odes... Written by Carl Anthony Waldron

NOBODY LISTENS

by Stephen Robert Sutton

Nobody listens
Nobody cares
Nobody wants to
Nobody dares

Frightened to speak
Left on the shelf
No one understands
My mental health

Vicious and spiteful
Echoes remain
No one is listening
To those insane

I speak of my illness
My problems in life
You cannot see madness
Not without strife

The darkness is present
The demons appear
You cannot see them
But believe me they're here

Nobody listens
To the words that I say
They think I am sane
But I muddle through the day

One day they will listen
And remember my name
Find my poor body
And say what a shame

Nobody listens
Nobody cares
Nobody wants to
Nobody dares

WHEN I FALL

by Stephen Robert Sutton

Who is going to catch me?
When I fall
Who is going to comfort me?
When I feel small

Are you going to find me?
When I am lost
Will you reimburse me?
For any cost

Are you going to forgive me?
When I do wrong
Are you going to sing me?
A comforting song

When I fall
Will you pick me up
Holding your hands
Like a plastic cup

Will you catch me?
When I fall
Will you make me feel
Ten feet tall

Will you pick me up
When I fall
Comfort me
When I feel small

Written about my childhood seeking help shouting into the wilderness, I hear my voice now and want to rescue myself from the past.

REFLECTIONS

by Stephen Robert Sutton

Reflections in the waters
The faces that we see
Made from our own memories
Looking back at me

Reflections in a mirror
An image of my face
With eye that are the mirror of my soul
Peer within my life is whole

Reflections speaks about myself
Like rows of tins upon a shelf
Each tin is part of my mind
With no empty ones you will find

Reflections based upon a time
When mother tells a nursery rhyme
Or father tells a fairytale
Of a dragon with a long sharp tail

Reflecting truth and fantasy
Telling what things used to be
Memories of a past concern
Is one way that we must learn

Reflections of my past looking back at the time of the covid 19 virus 2020

INTO DARKNESS

by Stephen Robert Sutton

Into the darkness I came to be
Into the darkness and looking at me
Seeing the person that I once was
Judging the person as anyone does

Helpless and hopeless I used to be
Acting so blindly unable to see
So weak in my mind and broken apart
I hear the sound of the beat of my heart

Anxious and nervous so much afraid
I wish someone would come to my aid
Help me to release all this pain deep inside
With no where to run to nowhere to hide

Fear is the enemy hope is the key
Chased by my past catching up with me
Into the darkness I hide my own past
Till someone finds me and frees me at last

In the bleakness of depression during the covid 19 corona virus 2020

MORAL GUIDANCE

by Stephen Robert Sutton

The course is set
For you to go
The destination
Is clear you know

Your parent or peers
Set the trail
For moral guidance
So don't you fail?

A blue print or map
Is drawn for you
Showing you
Just what to do

Whether it's straight
Or crooked you see
Follow the course
To what must be

Moral guidance
Is set from the start
So do you follow?
Your head or your heart

So follow your morals
And just you see
And just act
The best you can be

I LOVE MY WORRIOR (My daughter is a nurse and I wrote this after covid had arrived 2020) written by Robin Rich

They're choking on darkness
With no end in sight.
Afraid that they may
Be alone in this fight.

The captain is lying
And weapons are gone.
Yet weary from battle
They still carry on.

We worry and wonder
And ask ourselves why?
Not finding an answer
We look to the sky.

We cry, sometimes scream,
Beat our chest, pull our hair.
Oh God can you hear us?
Oh Lord are you there?

The enemy demands that
Our lives must be changed.
And the world as we know it
Has been rearranged.

Though lost in confusion
They're still standing tall.
A ship without compass
They answer the call.

Though the warriors are
Weary they have to prevail.
They're given no option
to win, lose or fail.

One day the enemy
Will have to retreat,
And having once fallen
We'll rise to our feet.

A new day is coming,
A new story to tell,
Of battle born warriors,
Who served us so well.

Robin Rich 2020

LOCK DOWN

by Stephen Robert Sutton

Here I am in a room
Feeling low full of gloom
This is what I see
The walls are closing in on me
Making use of the day
Families pass the time away
Being many or a few
They all find things to do
Children given little chores
And learn to play indoors
Home work takes part of the day
Baking cake for enjoyment they say
Families will swobble invading their space
All huddled together all in one place
End this covid virus some will pray
While some find activities best suits their day

Written at the start of the covid 19 pandemic 2020

PRAYER FOR RECOVERY

by Stephen Robert Sutton

I pray to god
That I survive
This awful virus
And stay alive
My friends have all been
Laid to rest
And live in heaven
Where they are blessed
Please let me recover
To tell the tale
I will always follow you
And never fail

Written at the time of the covid 19 pandemic

PANDEMIC

by Stephen Robert Sutton

Fear the virus
That comes your way
It's taking weak souls
The helpless this day

Thousands are fighting it
Its world wide you see
Its taken my friends
and its now after me

There is nowhere to run to
Nowhere to hide
It will surly get you
If you are outside

A pandemic attack
On hospital wards
We fight the attacks
By remaining indoors

Doctors and nurses
Are in the front line defence
Fighting the virus
Its so intense

So go to your homes
Just hide away
Come out when its safe
A much brighter day

Written from my experience of the Covid 19 pandemic of 2020

Wearing masks and two metre distancing and now read the following information

What is the velocity of a sneeze that's what you need to know and understand. Is it two metres or beyond this is vital information if you want to stay safe. Sneezes are speedy. "Sneezes travel at about 100 miles per hour," says Patti Wood, author of Success Signals: Understanding Body Language . She adds that a single sneeze can send 100,000 germs into the air. A cough can travel as fast as 50 mph and expel almost 3,000 droplets in just one go. Sneezes win though—they can travel up to 100 mph and create upwards of 100,000 droplets.9 Apr 2020

LIVING A COMPLEX LIFE

by Stephen Robert Sutton

Living life in complexity
That's what my life seems to be
With winding roads and a busy street
Nothing is straight, regimented or neat

With every day a complication
Try living life with such frustration
Roaming through life with no obligation
So much to do in my situation
Why can't I live with simplification?
Instead of a life of condemnation

Why my life can't be simplified
I want to run away, I want to hide
I sit with a blanket wrapped up inside
Shivering and rocking like my brain has died

And those dreaded days go on and on
I feel I have lost and someone else won
I am so tired I am going to bed
Lay down for a while just rest my head

The media offends me it depresses me too
I need a break so I am counting on you
Give me some good news fill me with hope
Uplift me I beg you please help me to cope

BUIDING YOUR LIFE WITH A SOLID FOUNDATION

by Stephen Robert Sutton

You are building your life
With a solid foundation
Living your life
Without complication

Building your life
With a foundation of love
This is built
By your parent with love

They supply you with
Religion and truth
Starting you off
When you're in your youth

Their political view
Reflecting on you
All their morals
Will follow you too

When you grow up
You choose your own way
And in your life
You hear what they say

Often we learn from
Our mistakes everyday
But we get through our life
In our own special way

HELPLESS

by Stephen Robert Sutton

I fell to the floor
Right next to the door
I had trouble getting up
And all I could feel was helpless

I fell down the stairs
And landed on the ground
Hurt my side
But didn't make a sound
But I was helpless

It's a well known fact
Many people have falls
Tripping over feet
And bouncing off walls
They are helpless

People in the park
And people in the street
Like homeless people
Those we often meet
Are helpless

FADED LIGHT

by Stephen Robert Sutton

Like a faded light
You appeared to me
With a boastful grin
Fading into iniquity

But your sins will get you
In the end
Like meeting
A long lost friend

Like a fading light
You came to be
A subject for
Controversy

This fading light
Is going out
And provide such answers
For those in doubt

Your religion
Will never save the day
Your thoughts will
Just simply fade away

PSYCHIC

by Stephen Robert Sutton

What do you see?
Through your special eye
An explanation
A reason why

The spirits seek you
To speak or chat
A psychic or clairvoyant
Where you are sat

Gifted with powers
To see what is to be
Unravel your life
Let us all see

The seat of a Wiseman
Dressed in dark clothes
Wearing tall spiky hats
And long hanging robes

You talk to the living
You talk to the dead
Some say its all happening
Others say it in your head

LIVING IN A BOX

by Stephen Robert Sutton

You live in the comfort
Of your very posh home
You will never be cold
You will never roam

While you enjoy all your food
Tuck into a roast
Discuss your income
Lets here you boast

So much rich living
Such comfort such ease
No one to think of
And no one to please

A man sits alone
His life in despair
No one to turn to
And no one to care

Cold dark nights in winter
Rain or even snow
With no one to turn to
No where to go

Living like an animal
Like a rabbit or fox
What life must be like
Living in a box

Plight of the homeless on the streets of Manchester

THE LOVE THAT NEVER WAS

by Stephen Robert Sutton

Like the flower that hardly blossoms
With a fragrance to admire
Or the fruit that just ripened
A taste you do desire

Like a sunset at the end of the day
This brings about the night
You dream about this moment
You live to see this sight

The one who is attractive
Is this the love that you desire?
The one that is so distant
Is she the one you admire?

Her eyes are blue and spark
Like diamonds in a ring
You want to tell her you love her
But you never do a thing

You love her soft complexion
Her hair of silk that does shine
You want to kiss her tender lips
To say she will be mine

But all you do is dream
And that is just because
She is with another man
She's the love that never was

PADDED CELL

by Stephen Robert Sutton

Listen to me scream
Listen to me shout
I am letting you know
That I am still about

Hitting all the walls
Swearing all the time
Bruising all my body
Isn't it a crime

I never knew what happened to me
I try to rationalise
Is it because I am mad
In this odd disguise

The madness is in my mind
Its started getting to me
Please get me out this padded cell
Come on set me free

WITCHES

by Stephen Robert Sutton

Witches fly high in the air
Witches dance without a care
They cast their spells late at night
And dance around under the moonlight

Witches cauldrons bubbling with the fire
They dance around and never tire
With cackling sounds they make a fright
Like owls that hoot throughout the night

Witches display magic at night
What a display, an awesome sight
Trick after trick, spell after spell
An incredible sight didn't they do well

Dark witches are legends white witches too
Showing the world all they can do
Halloween is the night for them
They can keep appearing again and again

WAKING BLIND

by Stephen Robert Sutton

The biggest shock to me
Happened when I couldn't see
I woke up blind one night
It was a dreadful fright

Not knowing what to do
What was I going through?
To this new life I appear
To live in mortal fear

No rhyme or reason I said
As I got out my bed
Reach out into dark new life
This is my horror it is my strife

Waking up to find I am blind
Or had I simply lost my mind
Stretching out my arms feeling for the wall
Frightened in case I had a fall

A teenager who had lost his sight
That was me and this was my plight
Not knowing how long it would last
Fortunately it is all in my past

EXPOSURE TO LOVE

by Stephen Robert Sutton

Give me your thoughts
Make it your goal
Open up your mind
Expose your soul

Give me your love
Day after day
Help me to live
In my own way

Cleanse all my thoughts
Open my heart
Then I will know
We will never be apart

Kiss my lips
Oh so tender
I love life
I live in splendour

I think about happiness
I think about love
I thank god
For my exposure of love

SENSELESS WORDS

by Stephen Robert Sutton

Voices drift
Within the air
People pass by
Without a care

Like an ever
Moving stream
It travels on
Like an endless dream

The sound does travel
On and on
And like the rain
Its come and gone

The words that leave you
Have been forgotten
Like unwanted food
That's gone rotten

The senseless words
Came from your mouth
They drifted north
And some drifted south

Carried forth
Within this time
They lost their purpose
As in a crime

Senseless words
Drift on and on
Never heard
Just by one

NAKED

by Stephen Robert Sutton

Stripped of my clothes
I sit naked in a room
A person with no purpose
Awaiting a pending doom

Vulnerable and alone
I remain naked on my bed
I reminisce my past
Thoughts within my head

Imprisoned by my past
In my naked state
Trying to keep my head
Considering my fate

I walk the street naked
Finally I am free
I look at others
To see my own vulnerability

CALM WATERS

by Stephen Robert Sutton

Calm my heart
Lift my soul
Bring me close
Make me whole

Calm my waters
By the stream
Calm my storm
Within my dream

Trust me with you
Be my mate
Calm my waters
Before it's too late

A chilled out look at life in a tranquil setting far from the hustle bustle of city life

FILL THE EARTH WITH PAGANS

there is a question
with an answer
that everybody's knowing
and that answer is
over seven billion
and growing
no need to count
it is official
so there can be no doubt

our Earth is over encumbered
by us useless eaters
over numbered
is the human race
a fact accepted
we see it for ourselves
and are told by teachers
no stats to leave repeaters

By Stephen Wright

ANCIENT RUINS

by Stephen Sutton

The sacred place for those
Who mourn their dead,
It concerns the fortress
Where lost souls do tread.

On the earth that speaks
to you of ancient times,
Of the battlement where
Soldiers committed their crimes.

The faith of god
knows no bounds
And the angels
with their spirits surrounds.

A journey through time
if you dare to see,
that age was a place
and time to be.

Searching souls for answers
of the lives once led
For the dead who
put their dreams to bed

Where disease and
poverty prevailed
And a hero coming
from battle was hailed

You now feel the chill
that lies in the air
That coldness is
like nothing to compare

But the ghost of
those left behind
Faint whispers
of someone confined

Trapped upon this earth
in the ruins of this place
You cannot see his image
you cannot see his face

You just feel his presence
as he passes you by
With a whispering voice
he never wanted to die

A maiden is also
dancing around
Singing so softly
its you that she's found

DREAM ON

by Stephen Robert Sutton

Cast your mind
Into the night sky
Its where we dream
Both you and I

Through the galaxy
In outer space
And there we will find
Our own perfect place

Beyond the planets
And the stars
As far as Jupiter,
Saturn and Mars

Through the black hole
A true phenomenon
Amidst all the stars
Where we are one

I dream of this place
Where we have gone
So every night
I say dream on

THOSE EYES

by Stephen Robert Sutton

Those eye that sparkle
Oh so bright
Those eyes that light up
In the night

Those eyes that tell
What you see
Those eye which express
The inner me

Those eyes that age
And fade away
Those eyes that
Have seen a better day

Those eyes that tell me
I am still whole
Those eyes are
My very soul

Those eyes that say
I do
Those eyes that say
I love you

PROFOUND THOUGHTS

by Stephen Robert Sutton

Deeply my thoughts are
A philosopher you see
Coping with life
With my degree

With my conviction
My obsession to study
I take my time
I am never in a hurry

My analysis is detailed
Examine the truth
A time for tutorial
While I am in my youth

By my motivation
Self evident I found
Constantly striving
Completely profound

Profound is my name
Because of my thinking you see
Striving to improve
A scholar I shall be

FREEDOM FROM BONDAGE

by Stephen Robert Sutton

I live my life totally free
But ask me where I want to be
Back in time just to see
The dreadful time of slavery
I would take an arm
Of the best fighting me
And rescue such slaves
And free all of them
Seeing the cruelty
Of the British Empire race
Wasn't it awful?
A total disgrace
They took from the country
And boasted with such hypocrisy
We would strip them of rank
And set the slaves free
It was a mockery
History clearly defines
And yet they were glorified
Or so history finds
Now we do find
The message is clear
Black lives matter
This we must cheer

WHIMPERED

Bead of perspiration a poet
Styling lines on hustler's head
Heading sweat shop on sun less day
Society is dead and who is dying for free?
What is freedom to no freeman?

Politrick sipping Moet before the figures of dust
Young gods digging dinner in the street of Kalahari
Tattered desert boot and ankle is shrinking
Few above many and pyramidal
Here is coldness and never spot Eskimos

Malcolm's way or dream a king?
Night sky assembly like Nat?
Can I paint happy faces with a fist in Soweto?
Hip Hop is trapped and where is the Emcee?
Still at the feet of pedagogue writing life.

-Thickcode

LEE

by Stephen Wright

I walk through Manchester city
the gardens of Piccadilly
town centre paradise
where some are trapped in hell
brown sugar and spice
the only souls to hold my eye
in any city
I guess it's seen in me
yeah they can tell
we've a little shared history

the boozers
the losers
substance abusers
we bow to no rulers
the system don't fool us
it's designed to confuse us
it's a sorry excuse yes
but we did not choose this life
it did choose us

a child approaches me
I smiled at him hopelessly
he's one of the lost
each other we've found
can you help me out
it will cost a brother a pound

all of his bare skin
is caked in shit
like he'd been working
naked down pit
twitching jerking
raging habit
eyes a glaze
eyes that says
his last month
blurred past like days

when I was seventeen
drugs to me was
ecstasy LSD buzzy bee
where's your party?
from where do you run son
what to you has been done
do you use to forget?
why is a child
consumed with regret?

I didn't get his name
sadly

there's another at home on the pavement
this one's more my age
forty
I stared at him at first in amazement
but my awe soon turned to rage
naughty

it was I that approached this vagrant
as I saw he surly had a story
more than worthy for the stage

he struggled to clutch
each vital crutch
I counted
drunkenly
two missing fingers on one hand
and on the other he'd lost three
for me that was too much
I shouted
tell me your story
did you once work in joinery?
the only such closely manicured paws
I saw before
was caused by circular saws

no
he told me

they were not lost to machinery
not perhaps like an ancestor
in the past there
spinning jenny
yet crippled just as viciously
as he slept
on the winter streets
of Manchester
I'd have no chance there

I doubted both
my lying ears
this affliction's for the pioneers
its only victims great explorers`
I was shocked to hear
it's happening here
as it is in the town next door yes
shamefully

on his right foot
I'm telling you
he had lost his every toe
the bloke poked
through his tattered shoe
to show so I did
know that it was true

I saw it
honestly
a glow in city lights
and no it's not a pretty sight
the brutal strike
of frost bite
hungrily
invisible teeth
in the darkness
inflicting grief
upon the homeless
on the streets beneath a

cloudless heartless night
mercilessly

I said I'm Ste
what your name be?
he said Lee
I said I'll tell people of you
Lee

Lee - a poem by Ste The Poet - All Poetry

- This definitely says a lot about society and the reality that a lot of people live in. There is pain, homelessness, sadness. You use so much description and I liked your use of few words on a single line. This poem flowed exceptionally well and was a good read.
allpoetry.com

THE LONELY NIGHT WATCHMAN

Dangerous they say
to wake a sleepwalker too soon
you are supposed to guide them
from living room

away from screen
unplug
it's only a dream
it's only a dream
repeat
the slipper slipped
then swapped feet
I weep for blood I dare not
wake from sleep

let them scream

for terrors of night
perpetual mare
may just have left the broken prepared
for what is come
goodnight our only Sun

By Stephen Wright

SUBSTANCE RECLUSE

by Wanda Bird

Think I'd be better off dead
So go on, pass me that redd
I won't suicide
So I'll get off my head

I'll get so fucked up
That the demons inside
Won't know whether to fight
Or just to run and hide

And for a few short hours
The pain is less
And my poor broken heart
Can deal with the mess

And when I come down
It can last for days
I get mental health issues
And live in a haze

Then I get back on my feet
And I'm forging ahead
I take a look at my life
And I break again

BIRTH AND DEATH

by Francis H Powell

You turned into an amphetamine
You were made of cellophane
Crystalline and gelatin
Sandwiched between a wake and a baptism
A fake and a giver of hope
You got out of your box
Totally intoxicated and unreasonable
You ran like a hound
Without co-ordination
You slithered and slumped
Draw faces in dust
Got bundled away
Strung up as a trophy
On the whispering walls
The pilgrim took time to muse
What had raddled the skyline
As he pondered he was wrestled to ground
And planted a seed to memories old and stained
And the jilted took their places at the wedding alter
And the maize grew strong in the wind.

TORMENTING SPIRIT

By Francis H Powell

Leave me alone you tormenting spirit !
How you tamper with air, water and all
The sustenance we feeble things require
Let me be released from my dismal memories
Liberated from their weight and burden
Your face comes in many forms
Your feet tread angrily on my bones,
As supple as delicate twigs,
After a rampant storm
You holler in the silence
Rattling the monotony
Like frivolity in a graveyard
Oh you churlish deceiver,
How could you take my time?
As if it were of no or little value?
Shredding my nobility
Cutting me down like a peasant
Salivating over his master's food
With a tirade of insults
Rasping his ears
Strange and different

AFRICA

by Francis H Powell

I have never been to India
but I feel like I have breathed
in the air, conversing with a maharaja
While on an elephant sozzled with gin
I have pranced on a delicate leaf
Written poems and shaved my head
I have never thrown a rotten tomato
at a politician on a podium
Or carrots at an insolent donkey.
Nor have I run with a pack of hyenas
Or counted up all my misdemeanors.
I have always painted with a fullness of heart
And respected others despite divisions
My mind has drifted to Africa, and dust filled Somalia
I have shivered in Siberia and sweated in Egypt.
When I depart this world,
My head will be filled with memories
Of places and people strange and different

TRANSFORMATION

by Kate Clayton

Transformation isn't always fragile,
Or beautiful as birds are free.
It's overindulging, insomnia,
Using your hand to suppress your scream.
Running to fast, or not moving at all,
Yet in the spaces between the deep breaths,
Cobwebs untangle and we find diamonds in the mess.
As ships don't observe the ground they cover,
But eventually arrive in new harbours.
So your soul is renewing and moving, and rocking,
So just be gentle dear child,
As you grow in the darkness.

Kate Clayton
@rubykatepoetry

SHOW ME

Show me how you love music, yet refuse to sing out of tune.
Show me how you love the stars, yet you despise the moon.
Show me why you love the city but beware you don't get lost.
Appreciate the stillness of mountains,
But don't focus on what they're not.
Tell me words of love and truth and speak with honest cause,
Take in all my beauty but don't rebuke my flaws.
Show me how to dance again, but sometimes allow me to lead,
Remind me how to harness the wind when my soul forgets to breathe.
Tell me how you paint the world when all is stripped away,
Remind me how to talk to God when I have forgotten how to pray.
Teach me how to love again but don't make demands on my heart,
Show me what is lovely, show me also, what is not.
Show me how to see again but allow me to shut my eyes,
Tell me the colours of your favourite sunset,
But don't discard my sunrise.
Show me how to walk with you but sometimes allow me to run,
Can we love and let love live,

When you show me you, and I show you me,
And our naked hearts journey on.

Kate Clayton
@rubykatepoetry

RIPTIDE

Indigo eyes that see into the future,
And as the rays of the summer sun beam into them,
It's like observing golden tigers dance in a field of asters.
Your beautiful mind runs like wild stallions,
Your hands have slayed dragons and harvested sugar cane,
They have also smashed the African coconuts and created dreadlocks
In your hair.
Your legs are strong, yet they know not how to walk,
Your wild hair has a dance of its own as you pounce from place to place.
It's like a tsunami married to a volcano watching you ravish life.
As if God placed some kind of raging ocean in your soul.
I pause to observe you embrace each moment of your awakening,
You make even watering the garden a tenacious war-cry.
Your heart wants to adopt orphans, and it is your heart that is beautiful.
When I feel like I cannot box in the storm that is you,
I will remind myself that you are every full moon I whispered to.
As I remove the thorns and twiggs from your hair,
and lay your exhausted body down to sleep,

I thank God He sent me a wild one,
He chose me to mother a riptide.

Kate Clayton
@rubykatepoetry

GOODBYE AFRICA

Goodbye my friend,
Thank you for birthing me and in doing so, you birthed my divine.
You will always be part of me,
And in every way possible I will call to you.
From far and beyond, through fingers that may tremble,
I will raise my hands and release to you my love.
Think of me Africa.
In every glorious sunset, and when you send your rain, know that I too am refreshed.
Oh how I shall miss your smell of dusty earth my beautiful friend.
When the eagles cry and the baobab trees rustle their leaves in response,
I too will sing in harmony.
When I run on new lands and swim in unfamiliar oceans,
they will feel the very pulse of a land within me so great,
That I fear the waters may just part.
People will observe where I walk,
and see my footprints shadowed by elephants and more and know,
That I have been one with the most sacred part of God.
I have slept in the very crevice of Gods heart,
And played in the earths most spectacular playground.
When I return, promise me that you will send me a hail storm,

And shower me with the essence of you.
My beautiful, beautiful.
Untamed Africa.

Kate Clayton
@rubykatepoetry

Kate grew up in Africa and now lives in New Zealand, she told me she loved Africa the scenery was breathtaking and that she found their was a lot going on there. She loved the wild life and writes passionately about the country

IMMIGRANT GIRL

Never before had she felt such trepidation,
No map could prepare her for this brave navigation.
To leave all She has, and all that She knows.
To find Her own truth and to then call it Her home.
To shelve Her dreams and bury Her plans,
As She embarks on this journey and discovers new lands.
She folds in her belongings, Her face rather militant,
The space that once stood a girl, now features an immigrant.

Kate Clayton
@rubykatepoetry

THE DARKEST OF DAYS

by Stephen Robert Sutton

I worship my love
And her wildest of ways
To lose her you see
Would be the darkest of days

She determines my thoughts
And rules my life
But never the less
She is my wife

Whatever she does
However she feels
Her every action
Always appeals

When I lost my heart
To that woman you see
I let it be known
I was as happy as can be

And now at her grave
I think of her ways
This is the worst time
The darkest of days

COURAGE

by Stephen Robert Sutton

I live my life
Without any shame
I lived my life
And played the game

I loved and laughed
My whole life through
And kept my cool
With so much to do

I was brave
In a times of concern
In living my life
With lessons to learn

My courage is there
for all to see
Through life's great battles
I came to be

Courage is shared
by a woman or a man
Whoever is like this?
I am their fan

Be it a man or woman
Their story is told
All of their life
Begins to unfold

SILENT WORLD

by Stephen Robert Sutton

No one knows
The way I feel
But in my world
You know its real

The silent world
I live my days
Without a sound
These are my ways

To see mouths move
Without a sound
Cars and buses
Moving all around

The birds are singing
Dogs bark out loud
Living in my silent world
Is really profound

I miss such a lot
Not hearing at all
I can't hear the clock
Ticking on the wall

We take for granted
What we hear and see
But just for a time
Please think of me

MULTI COLOURS

by Stephen Robert Sutton

I live my life in multi colours
May I explain to you
Like red yellow and green
Sometimes I feel blue

Multi colours explain the world
Like our society
Many colours like a rainbow
With so much variety

Colours are very useful
They describe my personality within
Often what I wear each day
Reflects the me within

Take the colour green
Like leaves upon a tree
We think of those who have the best
And are green with envy

The colour black is darkness
And white is so pure
Yellow is like yoke
A colour to endure

Red is for danger
So I heard it said
So take heed if you wear this colour
For it is you that they must dread

HOME BEFORE DARK

by Stephen Robert Sutton

I end my day at work
Time is getting on
I think about hours
Daylight will soon be gone

I race down the street
With my briefcase in my hand
Never stop to think
As I race right past the grand

I rush to the station
Running up the ramp
Donating all my change
To the homeless or a tramp

Rushing to the train
With the ticket in my hand
Dropped it on the platform
Where is it going to land?

I reach my destination
Hearing the dogs bark
I am glad I am back safely
Home before dark

FADED LIGHT

by Stephen Robert Sutton

Like a faded light
You appeared to me
With a boastful grin
Fading into iniquity

But your sins will get you
In the end
Like meeting
A long lost friend

Like a fading light
You came to be
A subject for
Controversy

This fading light
Is going out
And provide such answers
For those in doubt

Your religion
Will never save the day
Your thoughts will
Just simply fade away

PORTRAIT OF MY SOUL

by Stephen Robert Sutton

Paint a picture
On canvas for me
Using colours
That plainly I see

Dark colours of
Purple and grey
Depicting my mood
At the end of the day

Paint it in detail
Like a good photograph
Don't make it funny
Don't make me laugh

Make it so dull
But clear enough to see
Paint me a portrait
Do this for me

You are painting my soul
This looks very real
Paint me a conscience
So I can feel

Deep in my thoughts
I remember my pain
Scrub it all out
And start it again

RESCUE ME

by Stephen Robert Sutton

You reached out to me and pulled you out the mire
You poured water over me when you were on fire
You spoke to me when I were oh so low
You hurried me up when I was so slow

You calmed my waters cleansed my soul
I was so empty now I am whole
You instilled in me the chance of hope
Now I am so able to cope

You healed my cuts when I bled
You got some ice to cool my head
You fed me and gave me a drink
And when you spoke you made me think

Words of wisdom came from your mouth
As strong as the winds north and south
Gathers me up and whisks me away
Here I will fight another day

LIVING WITH A PHOBIA

by Stephen Robert Sutton

Rational fear is natural to us all
Like being on cliff top fearing to fall
Or falling in water thinking you would drown
Or on a ridge fright to jump down

But being frightened of a clown
Watching a show
Your friends want to see it
But you just want to go

Frightened of a spider or a mouse
Or of noises in your house
What is this irrational fear?
What is this coming near

But phobias are real to you
Who can explain what to do?
Coping with your own mind
With no explanation to find

THE EFFECTS OF FEAR

by Demi Tilsley

It's not a living thing
It's not even there
But lives in our heads
It makes us aware

Stops us from doing
Minds no longer clear
Takes so much from us
The thing we call fear

It takes away our breath
Leaves us paralysed
A mask upon the face
Our identity disguised

Like the beat of a drum
Heart starts pounding
Everything closes in
The walls that are surrounding

Sweat trickles down your cheeks
Words start to stutter
Hands & feet trembling
Stomach's got a flutter

It will take over our life
A head full of regret
Improve the way we think
Reform our mindset

So don't hold back
Consequences are severe
Don't let it control you
The thing we call fear.

By Demi Tilsley

GRIEVING

I'm sitting there contemplating
My eyes filling up with tears
I remember all those memories
We shared over the years

As I lie there wide awake
I'm staring into space
The images in my head
Are of your beautiful face

I'm feeling empty, sad & lonely
Emotions I can't control
Feelings I've never had before
In my heart you've left a hole

Even though I know its true
They say that I am grieving
I cannot help the fact
That I am disbelieving

I'm feeling so hurt
Feeling angry deep inside
You couldn't possibly imagine
How many tears I've cried

They say that times a healer
That you will start to be okay
I know that is not the truth
Whichever year or day.

By Demi Tilsley

THE REALITY OF MENTAL HEALTH

You put on a smile,
You act like your fun,
Your thoughts run away,
In your head you're all done.

You say you're okay,
You know it's a lie,
You get into bed,
Then that's when you cry.

You think you're being stupid,
There is so much frustration,
So you start to drift away
Into a world of isolation.

You're thinking way to much,
About life and our society,
All these thoughts in your head,
But you know it's this anxiety.
You can't shake it off,

And it won't go away
Yet you get up every morning,
And carry on with your day.
You're constantly tired, you struggle to wake,

You act like it's fine,
But you know you're being fake.
Falling asleep seems impossible,
Horrible thoughts in your head,
Why does it seem worse when you're lying in bed?

A heart that feels broken,
Holding back all your tears,
Standing and watching
Whilst your joy disappears.

Why is this me?
Why do I feel so alone?
All these questions I have,
But I don't like to moan.

You need to start living,
Time is ticking so fast,
Wasting this precious time,
Thinking you're an outcast.

You're blind eyed, you're in denial,
They start to ask questions,
So you run a mile.
You feel so rubbish,

Don't know what to say,
It'll get better, you hope and you pray.
The thoughts you think,
Are they real?

Will you live for tomorrow?
Will this be your last meal?
Can't sleep, can't stop thinking,
Smoking too much and too much drinking.

Feeling like a failure,
Maybe I took the wrong turn?
Your head starts to spin,
Your heart starts to burn

Looking in the mirror,
Staring at your face,
All you are seeing, is a massive disgrace.
Swallow the lump in your throat,

Wipe that tear from your eye,
Think of something else,
Don't you dare start to cry!
My life isn't that bad,

There's kids playing in the street,
With a growling empty stomach and no shoes on their feet.
So why am I hurting,
Can't stop these feelings that I'm feeling,

Depression go away!!
I need to start healing.
Life is a lesson, love & happiness we crave
We have to stay strong and try to be brave.

We can fight any battle,
Our minds they can torture,
I'm emotional,
Sensitive & a dramatic over thinker.
On my face I will smile but inside it's so dark,
My happiness has gone, there's no light without a spark.

Declining offers to socialise,
Using a lie for an excuse,
Torturing yourself is the worst kind of abuse.
It's time to speak up, it's now time to say,
It's ok to get help, there is always a way.

By Demi Tilsley

My names Demi-lea Tilsley, I'm 26 and married, I got married at 22. I live in Hednesford, Staffordshire.

In 2017 I was 23 and experienced loss for the first time, my grandad sadly passed away. I struggled with how to process it and ended up writing a poem about him, it helped a little writing down feelings. Ever since then if I ever struggle with anything I write it down using poetry. I also like writing about normal daily life eg. Fear, what is it to be a friend? Etc..
I attend church on a regular basis and have done missionary work in the past, I enjoy travelling to other countries. I work in the care industry working with individuals who have learning disabilities.

LET THE CANDLES BURN

Let the candles burn through the night
Let it burn now ever so bright
Let it flicker away but never ever go out
May it remind me to never live without a doubt

Let the candles burn and remind me of the truth
Of you and me when we were in our youth
Light up all the room with candles for each year
And may we think of a time when we would shed no tear

While the candle burn I will have company
Light those candles so I can see
Burn away in my room tonight
And forever make it bright

Burning softly in the breeze
Flickering candles putting me at ease
Slowly they go out one by one
Now I know that we are one

The candles were my burning life
Now they are gone I shall take flight
So let the candles burn in heaven instead
And put my thoughts and dreams to bed

ALL OR NOTHING

Put into life what you have got
Add in some more if you have a lot
Conjure ideas again and again
Keep on going tax your brain

Giving it your effort all your best
Put everything in and sod the rest
Give it your blood give it your soul
Give everything empty your bowl

Make all the effort to be a success
Don't hold nothing back or get in a mess
Follow your fortune follow your fame
Always remember be ahead of the game

Your talent is wasted while you are asleep
So use your time wisely life is not cheap
Be part of the stream flowing smoothly along
Be patient with yourself you can't go wrong
Its all or nothing people will say

MY BRAVE GIRL (GEMMA)

by Stephen Robert Sutton

The front line nurses
Prepare for war
With PPEs and
Problems in store

Battling the virus
Day after day
Defying all odd
And with them we pray

There with them
Goes my brave girl
All equipped
And in a whirl

She bravely fight
The evil foe
With all the knowledge
Set to go

Her mind is set
To do her best

To comfort some
And cure the rest

MY PERFECT WOMAN

by Stephen Robert Sutton

Your eye sparkle
Like diamonds in the sky
Those show compassion
Whenever you cry

Your smile
Lights up your face
I feel secure when you're around
Never out of place

Your hair shines
And flows down below your neck
Your skin is smooth
And is clear without a speck

You are so warm
And comfort me from the start
I feel you with me
Even when we are apart

You are so clever
Oh so very smart
I feel you with me
Close within my heart

GENDER CRISES

Who am I?
I don't know
Am I female?
Or just for show

Am I a person?
Who thinks and walks
Or a man
Who just thinks and talks

Am I a person?
Who questions my thoughts
Alters my body
From all marks and warts

Am I so weak?
Or am I so strong
Is it a problem?
or am I so wrong

I watch my body
I see it change
Is this unusual
Or is it so strange

Who am I?
And what is my sex?
What is my gender?
And is it the best

I want some answers
Please let me know
Give me some guidance
Let my life flow

SCARS

Be who you want to be
Do what you want to do
Live how you want to live
It's up to you

Forget what you need to forget
It's all in the past
Live for the present
It's with you at last

The scars do remind you
Of your past life that has been
Some scars are hidden
They will never be seen

Plan for your future
trips far ahead
But don't dream about them
You can't reach them from your bed

HOPELESS MESS

What sense is there?
In clouding your mind?
By destroying yourself,
Are you so blind?

You consume
Such stuff in your head
By the time you are twenty
You will surely be dead

You pollute your body
And strain your brain
You live in a box
Close to a drain

You sit by the roadside
With your head in a bag
And manage a breath
Between each rolled up fag

You drink from a bottle
Shared by a few
But as for clear thinking
It's not up to you

Your dirty mouth
Keeps people away
You had better start living
In a new kind of way

Come out of that dustbin
You look such a mess
Change your image
And become a success

Dope will never help
You to find a job or career
But it will end your life
Within a year

Empty lives
Produce empty dreams
Shallow heads
Without any schemes

Wisdom belongs
To those who can think
Haggled brains
For those who can drink

So wake up
When this nightmare ends
Who needs reality?
And who needs friends?

Logical thinking
Is far from your mind
Conquer your prison,
You are confined

You are a tramp
A modern day drop out
You are a mess
Of this I don't doubt

Your future died
When you were asleep
Now the frail weak body
Lies dead in a heap

MY FRIEND THE BOTTLE

Drink a glass
Of wine with me
Drink it down
Instead of tea

Drink a toast
to your lost friends
Have another
till the bottle ends

My friend the bottle
Is always by my side
My friend the bottle
Knows when to hide

My friend the bottle
Is close at hand
My friend the bottle
Is always in demand

So drink
To my health
Drink
To my wealth
Drink
To the birth of a child
Drink
Until you're reckless and wild

Drink
To a new life to begin
Drink
Whiskey or even neat gin

But then stop,
Be in control
Don't lose your character
Or public role

Think of others
Who may get hurt?
Why roll in the gutter
Or even in dirt

Are you that desperate?
To sink so low?
Or have you the will power
To just say no

DIARY OF A TEENAGE DRUG ADDICT

I wake up this morning
With my hair in a mess
I can't help it
Oh I couldn't care less

Yesterday was better
I don't know why
I feel dreadful
I just want to die

Just the other day
I had a dream
It was far out
I had to scream

A week a ago
I heard of a death
I have memories of her
It's all that's left

A single flower
Floats in a gutter
What a sad loss
Is all I can mutter

Cry after cry is all that I hear
From my hospital bed
Another mind is empty
Gone out of his head

DAMAGE

by Darragh McConn

Expectations mounting.
Shoulders crushing.
You either progress or you decay.
This is what pushes me.
This is what Haunts me.
Awards me.
Self critiquing for a millennia.
Getting fucked up for an era.
Borderline crossing nations to like schizophrenia.
My path is not one way or the other it is down the middle.
A black van pulls up.
3 men wearing balaclavas crash open the door.
Armed.
Steal your happiness, goals and glow.
Even with no grief.
Even through this ferocity will we still have self belief?
While people can mould and shape you telling you
you are wrong and incorrect eternally.
I don't want anything to do with what is right and the humans that believe it to be so.
An atheist.
But I have life beyond this outlet.
I prescribed myself escapism.
And I am doubling my dose.
Too many opinions I want no part of.

Choking from the throat on the embers of the past.
Trying to realize the power of the enabling of choice.

By Darragh McConn

THE WILDERNESS

by Darragh McConn

When you come face to face with your own mind.
Your own insanity.
Your own wildness within.
Primal eyes staring back at you in the dark.
But what are they seeking?
A fire lit torch illuminates the way through the subconscious.
Trudging through bogs of fire.
To finally.
To confront the wildness of within.
Born and bred into lunacy.
The wild is our first nature.
Running through your veins.
Past from generation to generation.
Surrounded by vicious predators.
Fights to the death under the new blood moon consumed by pitch darkness.
But I have not yet fallen.
Snakes forever slither through the tall grass.
Waiting for their chance.
But I just bought a lawn mower.
In some way everyday their will be something trying to take what's yours. Always with an ulterior motive.
One must remain calm.
They can smell fear.
A droplet of blood in the water echoes for miles.

But then you show them what you really are.
As soon as the blood turns cold.
The murderous mind becomes bold.
It is hard to be at peace when wrath lays upon your palms.
But it is down to us.
Who wins this day?
The light?
Or the dark?
Survival instincts.
Survival mode.
Muscle memory how we react.
Condescension spreads like a virus at times.
A vicious cycle we lay within.
And it does take its toll.
We survive the day and it all
Falls to us who you are upon the night.
It is down to humanity which way it decides to go.

By Darragh McConn

My name is Darragh McConn. I am originally from Roscommon town but now reside inGalway.

I got into poetry from a young age. Reading my Grandparents who was a Irish Speaking principal of a school

But I am self thought everything I know I know from research and practice writing. I write daily. It is an escape for me. From life for a while.

That is fantastic am very excited to see your finished piece. I will send on the auto corrected poems

BIPOLAR

The nights bleed into days, and sleep no exists
And the world seems cold as ice
No sleep…Thoughts …and negativity invades my
Mind…like a beating drum marching
To its own beat
The reflection in the mirror says this is you
But the smile I wear is a mask, and I am not what
People perceive
Two personalities are woven into one
Two bodies in one space that can't be done
Who am I?
Like demons and angels that fight among each other…
Both good and bad
An internal war…feeling both blessed and cursed
Resides inside me and there is no escape
Release me?
But there is no reply and the deafening silence speaks
Louder
Than any form of spoken words
Hidden from the world like a prisoner…locked away…
This battle is of my own, and only I can set myself free

By Tyeshia Sturgis 2020

Tyeshia is from Kentucky U.S.A, She has a passion for writing poems and has her own book coming out, she also write novels about vampires and such.

Tyeshia

I have grown as a woman over the past year and have accomplished a lot of my goals. During those times I've dealt w/men that never truly supported me but claim that they did... but thru my growth I've realized those men have no place in my life(I've let them go and I won't look back). I don't need anyone but me to make things happen. I'm going to continue to reach my goals and In the mean time...walk this journey alone. I'm going to wait on God's timing and lean upon him.

WHO AM I

by Tyeshia Sturgis

The words in my head
Slowly grinding at my mind
What is it, I needed to do

Several stories written before
None of them soothed my soul
But this time, things were different

And the emotions I head bottled inside
Needed for once, to be recognised
So I grabbed a pen and released it all

My paper used, as an outlet to speak
And then before I knew it, everything unfolded
And the world finally, knew me s a poet

Tyeshia Sturgis

DO YOU SEE ME

by Stephen Robert Sutton

Do you see me?
Do you care?
Am I invisible?
Just in the air

Do you see through me?
Like a ghost in the night
So do I scare you?
Fill you with fright

You walk right past me
Like I am not there
With no acknowledgement
Like you don't even care

You see only my fault
Like a lantern alight
Showing my madness
The goods not in sight

I look in a mirror
And I see my reflection
Is it really me?
Or just a deception

I want to scream
Just to be seen
Or trash everywhere
Just to be seen

Do you see me?
Could you just care?
Just speak to me
Make me aware

LIFE IS BEAUTIFUL

Life is beautiful.
Since *birth*, the *pain,*
Life *is beautiful.*
Growing up, the *rain*,
Life *is beautiful.*
Loved ones die, in *vain*.
Life *is beautiful.*
Lion sheds *his mane*.
Life *is beautiful.*
Children die, *some* slain.
Life *is beautiful.*
Along with, *your name*.
Life *is beautiful.*

My name is Daniel Baltazar Gorc. I was born in Czech Republic and live here my whole life so far, but I've never stayed in one place for too long. I've been a problem child and even failed high school because of drug use and mental health, which got me into a psychiatric ward twice before I turned 18. I managed to get my life on track (not back on it as it has never been there before), finished high school and now I am on my way to hopefuly get a doctorate in psychology and help people, especially like me, who often feel there is no way out and have nobody to confine their pain to in fear of being seen as insane.

I got into poetry as I began discovering my softer side through my development and were no longer hidden from the world, realising life not only got harder, but also much more beautiful than before. And one day I wrote a poem while on a walk through nature and I just never stopped since and even tho I dabble in several artforms none will be as close to my heart as poetry is.

LOOK

Look outside what do you see?
Marbles, trees or darkness close?
Perhaps you see just like me,
Perhaps we are stripped of clothes...
Perhaps we strip so easily,
We want our skin to breathe,
Perhaps we die so easily,
We know what it is to be.

THOUGHTS AND PRAYERS

Empty words, they perhaps shape,
More than one would think.
Everyday I pray with each blink,
To rid the world of needless hate,
Again with the empty words.
Nowadays it seemed like birds,
Hide more meaning in their chirps.

STEP

It takes takes just one and your life is gone,
it takes a thousand to get where you're going.
A step off course is a step on course,
if you can take the next one, of course.

I wrote one for you, it wasn't premeditated as almost
none of my poems are, but it came to me while working
and I had to take a minute

MR. SUTTON

Mr. Sutton seemed to live a life we'd all like,
A daughter or two, I'm not a stalking type.
I think he's lost more than most would hope to gain,
A nurse and a strong man,
Yet suffers from pain.
His work speaks to me from Manchester and beyond,
Senseless words to many maybe.
Yet he speaks to me through the senseless,
Sentences that blind the senses.
Gave me chance when none would listen,
Proved to me, somebody does.
And perhaps we can't hear each others deepest cries,
What matters to me: Someone tries.

Daniel Baltazar Gorc 2020

This means so much to me as a writer and humanist, I find Daniels work
interesting and very touching. He obvious is a warm deep feeling gentleman who
cares about others deeply. For this reason and for his poetry he is in my book.

TRANSITION (THE LINK)

by Stephen Robert Sutton

The link is between life and death
The moment you take your last breath
The transition of life existence
To the point of no resistance

The euphoria of a life beyond life
This place where you know you will strife
To the heavens that you may dream of
Far beyond the stars up above

Where angels glow an eternal light
And drift around in a heavenly flight
With the sound of an heavenly choir
This is where your spirit will retire

A journey from your own living soul
At last at peace, destiny is your goal
Far is the journey, but by the blink of an eye
You fade out and travel up past the sky

THE GHOST

by Stephen Robert Sutton

I speak to you
About the ghost
To explain it all
It's about a host

A man that carries
A deadly thing
A nasty virus
Or plague like thing

He makes his journey
Far and wide
With this deadly virus
Deep inside

He touches those
Who stand so close
This evil man
Who is called the ghost?

People die
A painful death
With burns and boils
And lack of breath

No one see him
Travelling near and far
But just leave them
With his deadly scar

The ghost could be
Standing by your side
You cannot escape him
You cannot hide

THE SLUG THAT ATE MY LETTUCE

by Stephen Robert Sutton

A slug just ate my lettuce
What could this possibly be
He ate the whole dam thing
And I wanted it for tea

He polished off my lettuce
That greedy big fat slug
Gobbled it oh so quick
Like I knew he would

That slug must have a death wish
I said with a tut
As I lifted up my leg
And squashed it with my foot

I am only kidding
All life is sacred to me
I let my little fat friend go
And had something else for tea

THE BIDDY MOBILE

by Stephen Robert Sutton

Going shopping is such a nightmare
Normally I wouldn't care
I like to shop and see the sights
But let me tell you about my frights

For most I know it seems okay
They can go shop for most of the day
But for the elderly I have to say
In their biddy mobiles they like to play

Yes mobile scooters are such a menace
I wish they would go to somewhere like Venice
Far away where the could do no harm
Let someone else have their biddy mobile charm

I dodge one and another comes along
Travelling past shops what could go wrong
I dodge another of those biddy mobiles
Then get caught under another ones wheel

They have stickers on the side of their scooter
Racing along and babbing their hooter
The sticker represents each person they hit
Every time they race past I have a fit

One day it will be me who will be a statistic
Hit by a biddy mobile and crushed like a biscuit
The driver proudly puts a sticker on the side
You have no where to run and no where to hide

WALKING MY HAMSTER

by Stephen Robert Sutton

I wanted to walk my hamster
So I asked my pet shops advice
He simply said how do you mean?
And oh that's rather nice

I said do you have a lead
That's small enough to work
I read the expression on his face
Suggesting I was a burke

I have no lead that would be so small
He advised laughing up his sleeve
It was like I was telling a joke
About something he would not believe

I can offer you a ball he said
Holding it in his hand
I really don't think he can play
Anything not even on command

You put your Hamster inside it
He said explaining how it would go
It's so he can run around safely
This you need to know

And so I felt more confident
As I took him to the park
He race around being chased by dog
And how they all did bark

Oh how I was grateful for this ball
It really changed our life around
Looking for the word to express it
It surely is profound

CHILDHOOD STRESS

by Stephen Robert Sutton

Listen to my sorrow
Listen to pain
Watch my stress
Its happening again

My chest is wheezing
I am out of breath
People frighten me
Half to death

The asthma is with me
Causing me harm
I want stop it
It's causing me harm

I can't stop it
It's causing me stress
I am in a state
Yes I am in a mess

So very worked up
I can hardly breathe now
Please tell me how to cope
Please show me how

No one understands
No one feels this way
I wonder how I make it
How I get through the day

I use inhalers
They stop this wheeze
With help from my parent
Who put me at ease

LIKE ANGELS DO

by Stephen Robert Sutton

I feel your presence next to me
An angel from above
I feel you're warm close to me
And sense selfless love

Your wings surround for protection
Your smile is their to see
I know you are my guardian
Sent here just for me

Your glowing light shows me the way
And sets a path secure
You guide me down that path so long
Because you're oh so pure

I pray that you stay with me
And guide me all my life long
With hopes and dream that keep me well
With an heavenly lasting song

So praise the lord that sent you
And makes you ever true
I always be a light for me
To shine like angels do

NOTHING IS REAL (PART 2)

by Stephen Robert Sutton

What is our perception of reality?
Our visual analysis of the facts presented
Is life really there in front of us?
Or is it something we have invented

Artifial intelligence created by man
A deception of the facts presented
Not real, but a project just artifial
But what we see is only invented

We are living our life
In a perpetual lie
We live out this act
And we eventually die

Every step every movement
Is planned from the start
Everything is timed
To the beat of our heart

What if we are
Just a part of the game?
With nothing explained
And nothing to gain
Just to win or lose according to chance
Like battle scene or prefixed romance

A journey through life
To see how we feel
No form of reality
Nothing is real

MANCHESTER AIR

by Stephen Robert Sutton

Arise arise to the Manchester air
Feeling free without a care
Breath it in within your skin
Just as you did when life did begin

All the races all of you kind
All your thoughts are brought to mind
Colour and creed are as one
Under the moon and under the sun

You working class have a place
All equal under Manchester's race
All alive and all do share
This our own Manchester air

We work together united in peace at this time
Live for a cause and don't commit any crime
And just as real as the stars above
We live for each other giving one love

Arise arise to the Manchester air
Feeling free without a care
Breath it in within your skin
Just as you did when life did begin

THE MANCHESTER BUSKER

by Stephen Robert Sutton

Standing alone in a street
Outside shops nice and neat
Playing guitar and singing out loud
She drew a very large crowd

The Manchester busker
As she became known
Performing for the crowd
Completely on her own

Her voice was heard down the street
Playing guitar tapping her feet
To the beat of a sound
People joined in all around

She played slow songs, fast songs
Rock and roll and rap songs
Reggae, blues and soul as well
Or ballads with a story to tell

The Manchester busker
As she became known
Performing for the crowd
Completely on her own

With her long dark hair
And a scarf round her neck flowing down
With a pair of ripped jean
She played her way across the town

SAD MEAL

by Stephen Robert Sutton

To eat a meal quick
Fast food is a way
It's nice and cheap
And fills you for the day

If you buy a happy meal
You're sure to be glad
You're thankful for
All the food you had

But if you get a sad meal
You get an empty box
I would say you'll be lucky
If you found some smelly socks

A sad meal will never fill you
I just like to see you face
To find your meal missing
It's lost without a trace

Of course I am only joking
Your meal is on the way
To see the look upon your face
It really made my day

JOURNEY THROUGH THE MIND OF A KILLER

by Stephen Robert Sutton

Take a journey with me inside the mind
You will never know what you may find
With narrow corridors full of light
Like lots of bulbs oh so bright

Here the deepest thoughts can be found
With such confusion the journey's profound
For here lies, the deepest secrets known to man
So try to solve it if you can

How the man first fell ill
Or why the man wanted to kill
Was he mad or was he bad
The story really is very sad

As his thought begin to unwind
We see what's in the real mind
In a dark room for hours he spent
Planning the evil of his own intent

With a murderous intention on his mind
With such brutality is what you will find
That journey you took inside his head
You were the victim and now you're dead

LOVE WITHOUT BOUNDARY

by Stephen Robert Sutton

Love is not far away at sea
It' never distant as far as you see
Loves never lost in a forest or cave
Or lost in a tunnel or a thing you can't save
Love is the sacrifice that you can make
Love isn't false, love isn't fake
Love is without boundary
Without barriers no lines are drawn out
I know when I love I am never in doubt
Love is so happy it brightens my life
Love says I want you to be my wife
Love is positive it's what we strive for
Love is the opening of every door
Love has no boundary no beginning or end
Love is your soul mate love is your friend
Love comes from the heart I know that my friend
Love is forever and it is a god send

VOICE OF THE DEAD

I wish these people would have told me, 'Rest in peace,'
while I was still alive, For many are the times I was in agony
And needed someone to show me love!
I wish these people would have given me a clothe
While I was walking naked in the streets of the world—
Then they would have restored my worth;
Do they dress me now to buy what they sold?
I wish these people would have cried for me in my life!
Then they would have dried up my tears.
Do they now shed crocodile tears or a devil's laugh
For wasting the chances they had with me all years!
I wish these people would have given me a place to lay my head
And shelter me from hostile weather and many other dangers
Rather than to dump me in a coffin when I am dead
While they neglected me as Christ was in the manger!
I wish these people would have visited me:
Coming so that we may commune with each other.
But now, whom are they coming to see
When we are separated far apart and not together?
I wish these people would have thanked God for my death.
They shouldn't mourn to the point of cursing
Him Since He taught me to number my days, gave me daily breath,

Peace in storms, and
NOW joy filled to the brim!

Poem written by Geoffrey Esilima, Kenya. He is the author of THE 7 WOMEN PLUS, THE LOST WORLDS and JOY & HAPPYNESS,
three poetry collections on Amazon Kindle

WESTWARD THE SIROCCO WINDS OF PLUTO MARCH

The scarlet flags swept across the land,
Turning the air mercurial and jaundiced,
And swept the tourists in its grains of sand,
Whirling as a fury as it kissed
Terra-firma draining the color from her lips,
Across the inter-continental expanse,
A cough, a sneeze, obsession eclipsed
Reason for the masked romance!
Shortages, businesses collapsed,
Opportunities lost to the savageness of the human race,
Who bleated in fear of becoming entranced
In fight or in flight from the savage shore and lost in space.

Scarlet flags swept the streets,
As in the ancient of days and Jericho's fiery aftermath
The mark of Cain upon our doors and upon our sheets,
That once safeguarded the way from the wrath
Of Samael's flaming sword,
Now affirm the children who bear the mark of death,
Blood pooling in lungs that sever the silver cord,
At the exhalation of expired breath.
Mind the medicum, and care for yourself,
For the compassion of the physician is sealed away
By the cold steel of clerical tongues.

Scarlet flags dress the horizon
Where we have retired to our homes, to isolate
Awaiting to hear the words of the most holy orison,
Will such words pass too late?
We isolate, as the hermit in the tall fields of wheat
Seekers of something tangible, something real,
Living in the shadows of the mercy seat
Where the world lives now, uploaded to a cloud of steel,
Virtual chaos, souls seeking meaning in the madness of the hour,
Flesh seeking a return to yesterday
Spirits in search of some stimulation to devour,
Who before were distracted by the lusty month of May,
See now the hell of the storm
With no sign of relent,
As we bear with marked faces, the viral form,
Our current, not normal, is only the present.

Bio: Katie Anderson is a scholar and poet living in the United States. Her poems have appeared in *The Diviner's Handbook: Ancient and Modern Practices of Divination* and *Celebrating Poetry: Saint Louis County Library.* http://rosalvastudio.wordpress.com

OTHER BOOKS WRITTEN

OUT OF THE JAR –MY BOOK OF POEMS

DEEP IN THOUGHT –MORE POEMS FROM THE JAR

EIGHT SKULLS OF TEVERSHAM

STORIES BEYOND BELIEF

STORIES BEYOND BELIEF TWO

CRACKED PORCELAIN FULL STORY

CURSED Simon Robert Sinclair

CRACKED PORCELAIN – ACTS OF ABUSE Sarah Ruth Scott

STEPHEN SUTTON

DEEP in THOUGHT

MORE POEMS FROM THE JAR

OUT OF THE JAR
MY BOOK OF POEMS

STEPHEN ROBERT SUTTON

Chocolate Candy Always Melts In The Sun

TYESHIA STURGIS

THE 7 WOMEN PLUS

Geoffrey Esilima

Behind
The MASK

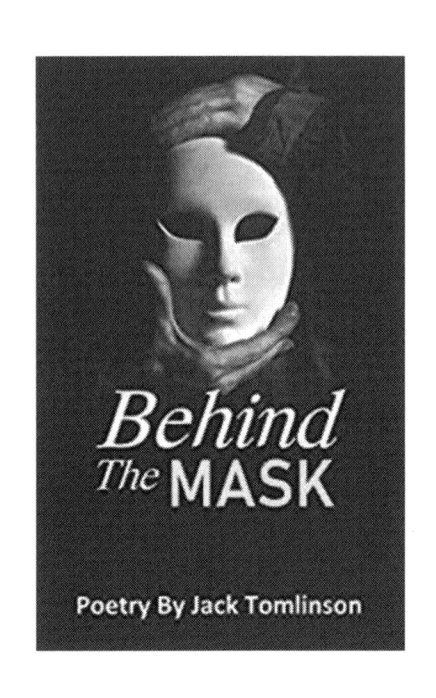

Poetry By Jack Tomlinson

Printed in Great Britain
by Amazon